Contents

Words in **bold** are explained
on pages 30 and 31.

What is summer?

Summer is the hottest time of the year. It's sunny and warm, and the air is full of buzzing insects and the smell of flowers.

Spring

In summer, schools close for the long summer holidays. It's time to play! People go on holiday to the seaside. Roads, railways and airports are very busy.

Summer is a time for going outdoors. You can go for a walk, play games or paddle at the seaside.

summer fact

You should never look directly at the Sun. It could damage your eyes or even blind you.

4

Summer

Autumn

Winter

Red poppies **bloom** in summer. Sometimes there are so many of them, they look like a red carpet.

Summer is one of the four seasons: spring, summer, autumn and winter. Together the four seasons make up the whole year.

Flowers bloom and bees buzz around them, collecting **nectar** and **pollen**. The trees are covered with lush, green leaves. They give shade from the hot Sun.

How summer happens

Wherever you live, summer is warmer than any other season. But do you know why?

The Earth is always moving around the Sun in a big circle. It takes a whole year to travel all the way around.

The Earth is tilted to one side. As it moves round the Sun, the tilt makes different parts of the Earth face the Sun at different times. This is why we have seasons.

This picture shows the seasons in the **northern hemisphere**.

Summer happens when the part of the Earth you live in leans towards the Sun.

Winter happens when your part of the Earth is leaning away from the Sun.

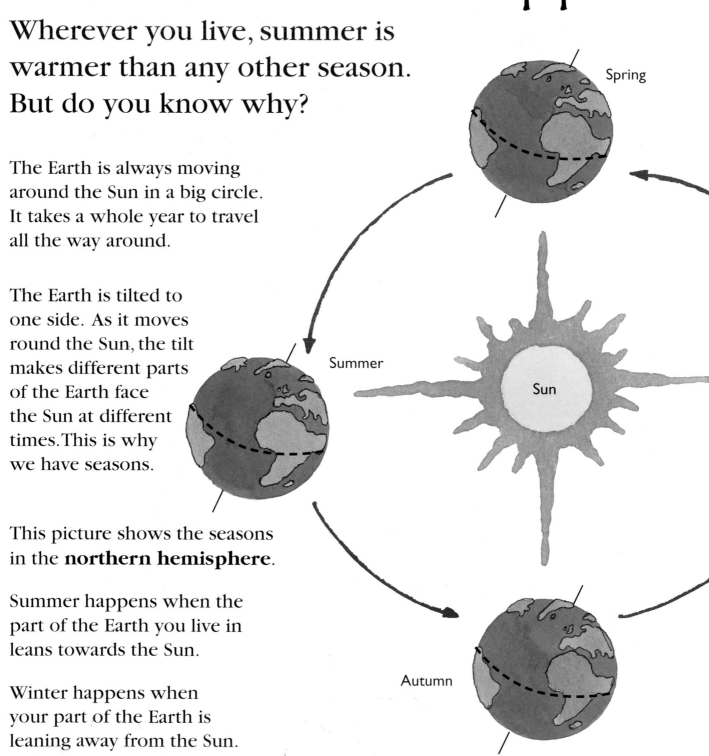

Spring

Summer

Sun

Autumn

If you live in the northern hemisphere, or northern half of the Earth, it's summer when the **North Pole** is tilted towards the Sun. The days are long and sunny and the nights are short.

If you live in the **southern hemisphere**, summer is when the **South Pole** is tilted towards the Sun.

North Pole

Northern hemisphere

Equator

Southern hemisphere

South Pole

Winter

summer fact

At lunchtime on a summer day, your shadow looks very short. This is because the Sun is high in the sky.

Do you like playing outdoor games in summer?

In summer, the daylight lasts longer than in winter. It may still be light when you go to bed.

Around the world

Summer doesn't happen at the same time all over the world. If you live in America, Europe, India or anywhere in the northern hemisphere, summer is in June, July and August.

But in the southern hemisphere, in South America or Australia, summer is in December, January and February.

Some countries are very wet in summer. In India and other parts of Asia, the rainy **monsoon** season starts in July. The rain means crops and animals will have enough water. But it can cause floods too.

A monsoon rainstorm in the Philippines.

North Pole

Equator

South Pole

At the North and South Poles, there are summer days when the Sun never sets and there is no night. The countries around the North Pole, such as Greenland and Iceland, are sometimes called the Land of the Midnight Sun.

In Australia, Christmas Day is usually hot and sunny. But many Australians still have snow decorations and pictures of Santa on a sleigh!

Husky dogs asleep at midnight in Greenland.

Summer weather

Many summer days are warm and sunny, with a gentle breeze to keep you cool. The Sun feels hot in summer because it's closer to us than at other times of the year.

Is there a cloud in the sky? If there is, it's probably a light, white, fluffy **cumulus cloud**. Cumulus clouds float high up and hardly ever turn into rain.

We eat cold food like ice cream and ice lollies to keep us cool.

If the sky looks dark and gloomy, there may be a **thunderstorm**. You might hear a crash of thunder and see a flash of lightning, followed by heavy rain. Lightning can strike trees and buildings.

summer fact

A lightning strike contains as much electrical power as 2½ million light bulbs!

Sometimes, summer weather is **humid**. There is no wind, and the air feels heavy, warm and damp.

Summer weather can sometimes be rainy and sunny at the same time!

11

Plants in summer

Roses, daisies, buttercups and lots of other flowers bloom in summer.

Flowers need to make seeds so that new plants can grow. A special dust inside the flower called pollen travels from one plant to another. When the pollen lands on another flower, a new seed is made.

If you looked at a flower under a microscope you would see tiny grains of pollen like this.

Many flowers have a lovely smell and contain a sweet juice called nectar. Bees and other insects smell the scent and come to collect the tasty nectar. At the same time, they carry pollen from one flower to the next.

A meadow full of sweet-smelling flowers attracts many insects in the summer.

Plants soak up light from the Sun in their leaves. The leaves use the sunlight to make food for the plant, using water from the soil and carbon dioxide from the air. This is called **photosynthesis**.

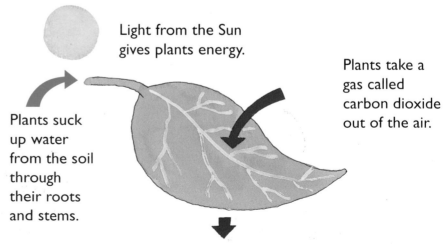

Light from the Sun gives plants energy.

Plants take a gas called carbon dioxide out of the air.

Plants suck up water from the soil through their roots and stems.

When a leaf is making food, it breathes out a gas called oxygen.

Insects like this swallowtail butterfly love to drink the sweet nectar from flowers.

summer fact

If you have hayfever, summer makes you sneeze! This happens because pollen floating in the air tickles the inside of your nose.

Animals in summer

There are more animals around in summer, because there are lots of leaves and flowers for them to eat.

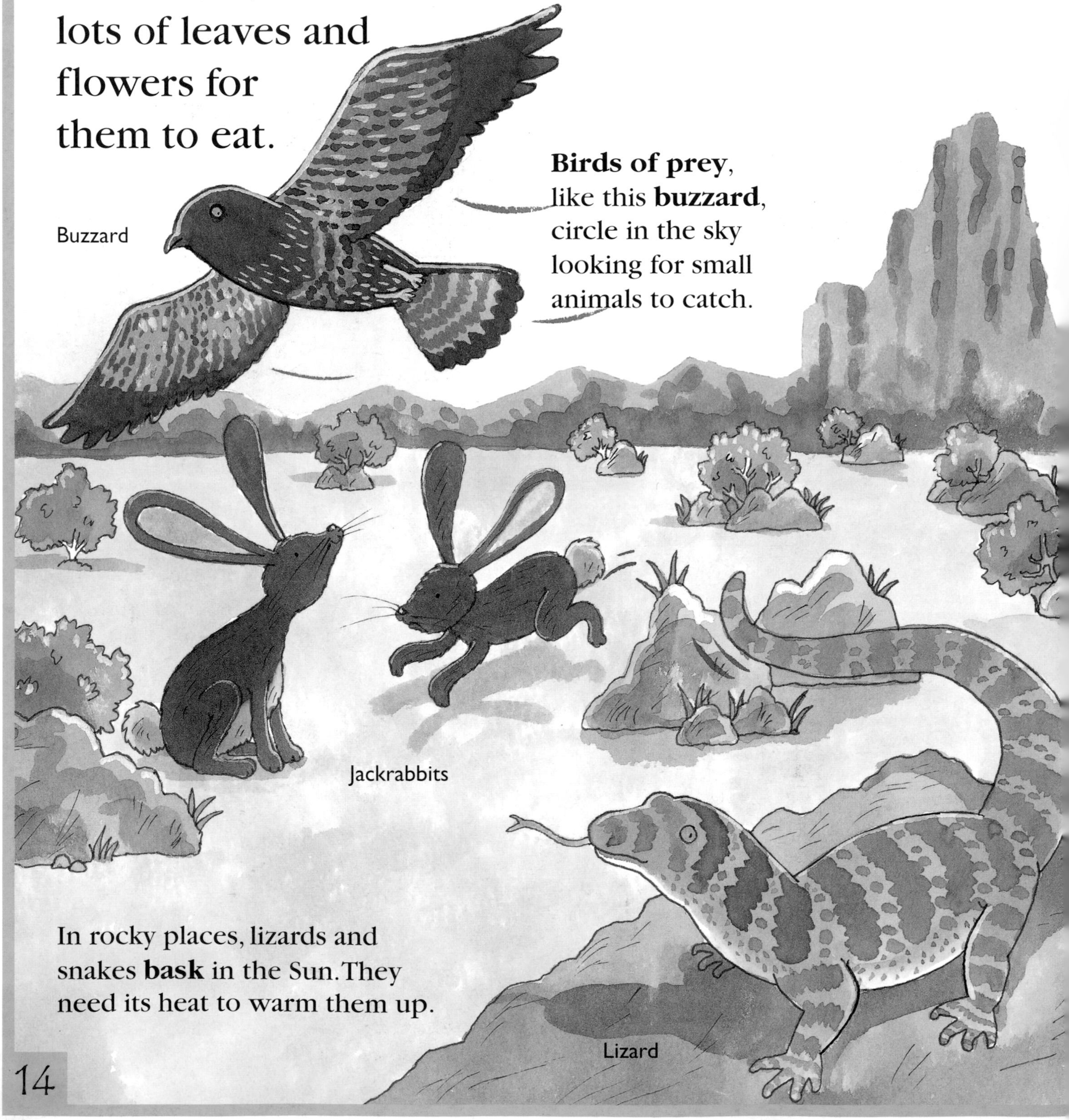

Buzzard

Birds of prey, like this **buzzard**, circle in the sky looking for small animals to catch.

Jackrabbits

In rocky places, lizards and snakes **bask** in the Sun. They need its heat to warm them up.

Lizard

Bees spend the summer collecting nectar from flowers and turning it into honey. They store the honey so they will have food for the winter.

Some animals can feel too hot in the Sun. They need to cool down. Penguins don't like the heat. They spend summer days in the water and only come ashore in the evening.

King penguins coming out of the sea.

summer fact

During the summer, birds replace all their feathers! The feathers fall out two at a time, and new ones grow in their place.

On hot, sunny days, birds splash in streams and bird baths to cool down.

On the farm

Summer is a busy time for farmers. Their crops are growing tall and ripe, ready for the **harvest**. But that means birds, insects and other animals will try to eat them. How can farmers keep their crops safe?

Some farmers put hunting insects, such as ladybirds, in their fields. The hunters eat the smaller insects that feed on the crops.

Farmers often spray their crops with chemicals called pesticides. They keep crops safe by killing insects.

A helicopter sprays pesticide on apple trees.

In some hot places, such as Israel and Australia, farmers have to water their crops to make sure they don't die. This is called irrigation.

The plants in this nursery are watered with sprinklers.

Farmers put scarecrows in fields to frighten birds away. But the birds soon get used to them!

summer fact

When sunflowers are growing, they turn to face the Sun as it moves across the sky.

People in summer

Summer means fun! It's time to play outside, have picnics and go to the seaside.

Roads and airports are very busy, because so many people go on holiday at the same time.

These boys in Saudi Arabia wear white shirts that help them stay cool in the hot Sun.

Some people have **barbecues** in the garden.

summer fact

Wearing white or pale clothes keeps you cool, because the colour **reflects** the Sun's heat.

Gardeners mow their lawns and water their plants.

18

It's great fun playing in a paddling pool or having a water fight.

What special clothes do you wear in summer?

When it's really hot, all you want to wear are shorts and a T-shirt, or a sundress.

But the Sun can dazzle your eyes. A sunhat and sunglasses keep you in the shade.

Sandals or flip-flops let your toes stay cool.

Your body uses sunshine to make vitamin D. This vitamin helps to keep your bones and teeth strong.

Summer festivals

Midsummer is a holiday in many countries in the northern hemisphere. Midsummer's Day is on 21 June.

Some people like to stay up all night and watch the sun rise on midsummer morning.

summer fact

In Finland, the midsummer **festival** is marked with bonfires, flower decorations and waving flags.

In America 4 July is Independence Day. People celebrate the day when America stopped being ruled by Britain, and became a free country. There are street parties with fireworks and marching bands.

A powwow dance in Washington, USA.

Native Americans hold festivals called powwows in summer. At a powwow, there are games and sports, and **traditional** music and dancing. Powwow dancers wear costumes made of feathers.

Summer long ago

On a hot summer's day, everyone wants an ice cream or a cold drink from the fridge. But long ago, there were no electric fridges or freezers!

Instead, food was kept cool using ice from ice farms. These were farms where ice was collected in the winter and stored in a barn. In summer you could buy a block of ice and put it in your ice box – a kind of early fridge. The ice slowly melted as the summer went on.

These people, called Druids, meet at Stonehenge every year.

Prehistoric people celebrated midsummer. We can tell this from ancient stone circles such as Stonehenge in England. It is built so that the Sun shines through a gap in the stones on the morning of Midsummer's Day.

The Aztecs, who lived in Mexico about 500 years ago, believed the Sun was a powerful god. They worshipped him all year round, but especially at midsummer. They made human **sacrifices** to keep the Sun god happy.

An ancient Aztec temple in Mexico.

summer fact

Some Aztec people still live in Mexico. They welcome the **summer solstice** by banging drums and shaking rattles.

23

Summer dangers

Have fun in the summer, but watch out! The Sun and the seaside can be dangerous. But you can stay safe.

If you stay out in the Sun for too long, you might become sunburned. Your skin will look red and feel sore. Sometimes the sore skin peels off.

Rub suncream on your skin to stop sunburn.

Wear a hat and a T-shirt to keep the sun off.

If you are sunburned, stay in the shade.

At the beach, strong **currents** can sweep swimmers out to sea. Lifeguards keep watch at the seaside so they can rescue anyone who's in trouble.

Don't swim near sharp rocks like these!

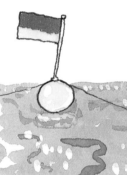

Flags like these show you where it's safe to swim and paddle.

If the weather is very hot and dry, there is a **drought**. Crops can't get enough water, so they wither away and die.

Sunflowers drooping in a drought.

25

Summer activities

Here are some activities to do in summer.

When you're getting ready for a picnic, try these ideas.

Make quick picnic 'sausages' by rolling up a piece of ham or lettuce and a cheese slice inside a piece of soft sliced bread.

Use a cocktail stick to keep them rolled up until you eat them.

Put ice cubes in your juice or lemonade. By the time you have your picnic, the cubes will have melted, but your drink will be ice-cold.

If you have a garden, why not eat outside?

You've probably thought of making a sandcastle when you're at the beach. But how about making something else? Here are some ideas.

A sandman is like a snowman, but made out of sand. You could use shells or pebbles for his eyes and nose. Ice lolly sticks make great spiky hair.

Shells make great sandcastle decorations.

Build a sand boat or car that you can sit inside. Make a control panel out of shells and stones.

Summer experiments

Disappearing tricks

When you hang washing out to dry in the sun, where does all the water go?

It turns into a gas called water vapour and floats away into the air. This is called **evaporation**.

Try this experiment. It works best on a really hot day.

Pour about half a cup of water on a hard, flat, dry patch of ground.

When the water has spread out, draw around the wet area with a piece of chalk.

After a few minutes, look at the chalk mark again. Is the area inside it still all wet?

Some of the water has gone because it has evaporated into the air. The heat from the Sun and the ground turn the water into **vapour**.

Pupil test

Your **pupils** are the black dots in the middle of your eyes. They are holes that let light into your eyes, so that you can see.

In bright sunshine, your pupils become smaller so that they don't let in too much light.

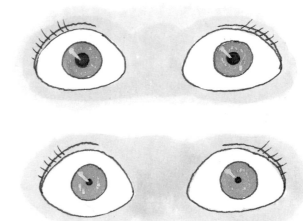

Try this experiment with your friends when you're outside on a sunny day.

Ask your friends to shut their eyes and cover them with their hands for a few seconds.

Then ask them to take their hands away quickly and open their eyes, while you watch closely.

Can you see their pupils shrink when they sense the bright sunshine?

29

Words to remember

buzzard
A kind of bird. Buzzards hunt other birds and small animals.

barbecue
A grill for cooking food outdoors.

bask
When an animal basks, it lies in the Sun to get warm.

bird of prey
A bird that hunts and eats other animals.

bloom
When a tree or plant blooms, its flowers come out.

cumulus cloud
A white, fluffy cloud which you can often see in summer.

current
A stream of moving water in a river or in the sea. A strong current can sweep you away.

drought
Very dry weather with little rain.

equator
The line around the middle of the Earth. There is no real line there – it is drawn on maps and globes.

evaporate
When water evaporates, it changes from a liquid into a gas and escapes into the air.

festival
A party or feast to celebrate a special date.

harvest
The time when farmers collect, or harvest, their crops.

hemisphere
One half of the Earth.

humid
When the air is very still, and feels warm and damp.

monsoon
A summer wind that brings heavy rain to India and nearby countries.

Native Americans
The people who lived in America before explorers arrived from Europe.

nectar
A sweet juice found inside flowers.

northern hemisphere
The northern half of the world, where Europe, America and Russia are.

North Pole
The most northern place on Earth.

photosynthesis
The name for the way plants turn sunlight into food inside their leaves.

pollen
A fine yellow powder made by flowers.

prehistoric
From the time before history started to be written down.

pupil
The round black hole in the middle of your eye.

reflect
When something reflects heat or light, it means that heat or light bounces off it.

sacrifice
To give up something for someone else. Long ago, people used to make human sacrifices, which meant they killed other people to make their gods happy.

southern hemisphere
The southern half of the world, where Australia is.

South Pole
The most southern place on Earth.

summer solstice
The longest day of the year, when your part of the Earth is leaning most towards the Sun.

thunderstorm
A storm with thunder, lightning and heavy rain.

tradition
Something people have done for a long time.

water vapour
The name for water that has turned into a gas.

Index